Hiking

By Kristin Thoennes Keller

Consultant:
Elizabeth Dooley
Alliance Programs Coordinator
American Hiking Society

CAPSTONE
HIGH-INTEREST
BOOKS

an imprint of Capstone Press
Mankato, Minnesota

Capstone High-Interest Books are published by Capstone Press
151 Good Counsel Drive, P.O. Box 669, Mankato, Minnesota 56002
http://www.capstone-press.com

Library of Congress Cataloging-in-Publication Data
Thoennes Keller, Kristin.
   Hiking/by Kristin Thoennes Keller.
   p. cm.☐(The great outdoors)
   Includes bibliographical references and index.
   ISBN 0-7368-0916-3
   1. Hiking☐Juvenile literature. [1. Hiking.] I. Title. II. Series.
GV199.52 .T46 2002
796.51☐dc21   00-012550

Summary: Describes the equipment, skills, safety issues, and environmental concerns
of hiking.

Editorial Credits

Carrie Braulick, editor; Lois Wallentine, product planning editor; Timothy Halldin,
   cover designer and illustrator; Katy Kudela, photo researcher

Photo Credits

Capstone Press/Gary Sundermeyer, cover (bottom left, bottom right), 7, 11,
   16 (foreground), 21 (foreground), 22, 28, 31
Comstock, Inc., 1, 16 (background), 21 (background)
Jeff Henry/Roche Jaune Pictures, Inc., 25, 33
Jeff March Nature Photography, 41
Jon Gnass/Gnass Photo Images, 34
Kathy Adams Clark/KAC Productions, 38 (top)
Kent and Donna Dannen, 8
Photo Network, cover (top right); Photo Network/Henryk T. Kaiser, 14
Photri-Microstock/C. W. Biedel, M.D., 39
Rob and Ann Simpson, 42
Tom Devol/Gnass Photo Images, 12
Unicorn Stock Photos/Rod Furgason, 36
Visuals Unlimited/Mark E. Gibson, 4; Mark S. Skalny, 19; Robert Gustafson,
   38 (bottom)

1 2 3 4 5 6 07 06 05 04 03 02

Table of Contents

CHAPTER 1

Hiking

People have hiked throughout history. Cave drawings from prehistoric times show people walking to find food and shelter. Ancient Greeks and Romans often held meetings while they walked. Today, most people hike for recreation.

Recreational Hiking

People hike for various reasons. Some people hike for exercise or to spend time in nature. They may hike to spend time with family or friends. Many people enjoy the physical and mental challenges of hiking.

Some hikers carry camping equipment in backpacks to stay overnight outdoors. This type of hiking is called backpacking. Other

Many people hike for exercise and to spend time with others.

hikers complete their hike in one day. This activity is called day hiking.

Hiking Areas

Hikers can walk in a variety of areas. Most people hike near wilderness areas. They may hike near rivers, lakes, or mountains.

Hikers walk on a variety of terrain. They may hike on low, rolling hills. They may walk over sand in the desert. Some hikers walk on scree. This loose, rocky terrain covers many mountainsides and steep hills.

Most hikers walk on trails. State and national parks often provide trails for hikers. Nature centers and local governments also may provide hiking trails. Some hiking organizations build and maintain their own trails.

Signs mark trails for hikers.

Hikers can adjust the straps on day packs to make them more comfortable to wear.

5 miles (8 kilometers) they plan to hike. Hikers should stop often to drink water. They should drink before they become thirsty to prevent dehydration. People who are dehydrated do not have enough water in their bodies. They can become very sick. Hikers in extremely hot or cold weather should drink extra water. These hikers should carry at least 1 gallon (3.8 liters) of water.

Hikers can use a filter to purify water from natural sources.

Some hikers plan to walk near natural water sources such as streams or ponds. These hikers may carry less water with them. Instead, they carry equipment to purify water from natural sources. This water often contains germs that can make people sick. The hikers may run the water through a water filter to purify it. They also may use iodine tablets, crystals, or drops to treat water. Some hikers boil the water in a pan for three to five minutes to purify it.

Hikers should bring food to help them maintain their energy levels. The food should stay fresh during the hikes. Hikers should stop every one or two hours to eat. Many hikers bring high-energy food such as beef jerky or peanuts. They also may bring fresh or dried fruits. Cheese sticks and sunflower seeds also are suitable food choices for hikers.

Useful Equipment

Hikers carry certain equipment. They should have a map of the area and a compass to help them keep track of their location. Many parks and hiking organizations have maps of trails. Most of these maps are topographical. These maps show an area's surface features. These features include rivers and mountains. The maps have curving lines called contours to show the height of certain areas.

Wristwatches help hikers know when to begin their return hike. Hikers should make sure their watches have new batteries.

Some items are necessary for emergencies or unexpected situations. For example, hikers may become lost and remain on a trail after it becomes dark. Hikers should carry firestarter or

A compass can help guide hikers as they travel.

waterproof matches. Hikers may make a fire
with these items to keep warm, signal others,
or to cook. They should keep these items in a
waterproof container. Hikers also should carry
a flashlight with new batteries.

Hikers should have a whistle and a
pocketknife. A lost hiker can blow the whistle
to alert others. Hikers can use a pocketknife to
cut a bandage or untie a knot.

Some hikers carry money. They may need money to make a phone call or buy additional food during an emergency.

Hikers may bring binoculars. These viewing instruments allow people to observe objects from a distance.

Hikers should carry a first aid kit in case of injuries. They may put together their own kits or buy them at department or outdoor stores. Hikers should carry a snake bite kit in areas where venomous snakes live. These snakes produce poison. People who are bitten by venomous snakes can become sick or die.

Some hikers buy hiking sticks at outdoor stores. These sticks usually are made of wood or a lightweight metal. Hikers use hiking sticks for support and balance on rough terrain.

Clothing

Most people hike during seasons of mild weather instead of winter. But the temperature often changes throughout the day. Hikers should dress in layers. They can add or remove layers to quickly warm or cool their body temperature.

Gorp

Many hikers bring a mixture of foods called gorp on their hikes. This mixture provides energy for hikers. Some people say gorp stands for "granola, oatmeal, raisins, and peanuts." Others say it stands for "good old raisins and peanuts."

Ingredients:

1 cup almonds
1 cup banana chips
1 cup cashews
2 cups toasted oat cereal
1 cup chopped dates
1 5-ounce package of
  dried apples
1 cup figs
1 cup macadamia nuts

1 cup coated chocolate candies
1 cup oatmeal
1 cup peanuts
1 cup pecans
1 cup prunes
1 cup raisins
1 cup shredded coconut
1 cup sunflower seeds
1 cup walnuts

Equipment:
Large bowl
Large spoon
Plastic bags or containers

1. Combine all ingredients in a large bowl.

2. Mix ingredients together with a large spoon.

3. Divide into plastic bags or containers for packing.

The layer of clothing next to the skin should keep hikers dry. Hikers usually choose a fabric that draws moisture away from the skin. A synthetic fabric made from polyester such as polypropylene is a good choice for this layer. Synthetic fabrics are made by people. Other hikers choose wool for the first clothing layer. This fabric keeps hikers warm even when it becomes wet.

Hikers should not wear cotton clothing such as jeans. Cotton stays wet for a long period of time. It can make hikers cold and uncomfortable.

The middle layer of clothing should keep hikers warm. It also should move moisture outward. Many hikers prefer a warm, lightweight fabric called fleece for this layer. Fleece allows sweat and body odors to pass through to the outer layers.

Hikers' top layer of clothing should be windproof and water-resistant. Hikers should have a breathable jacket. The jacket's fabric should allow air to pass through it. This feature helps prevent hikers from becoming too warm. Many hikers wear nylon jackets. Some hikers wear polypropylene pants.

Some hikers bring a breathable nylon waterproof jacket in case of heavy rain. Jackets that are not breathable should have slits to allow air to pass through.

Some hikers bring a change of clothing. They change into dry clothing if their other clothing becomes wet.

Footwear

Hikers need proper footwear. Many people wear hiking boots. Hiking boots have thick soles and deep grooves to help hikers grip surfaces. Some hikers wear sneakers or other types of walking shoes. These hikers usually hike on flat, smooth terrain.

Hikers choose boots or shoes that fit comfortably. Shoes that are too tight can cause hikers' feet to become sore. Hikers should break in new footwear. They should wear the boots or shoes for several days before hiking. This activity allows the footwear to conform to the shape of hikers' feet.

Experienced hikers usually wear wool socks or socks made of synthetic fabric blends. They

Hiking boots are sturdy and have grooves to help hikers grip surfaces.

do not wear cotton socks. Hikers' feet often perspire and form moisture. Cotton often stays wet. The wet material can rub against the skin and cause blisters on hikers' feet. These bubbles of skin filled with liquid usually are painful. Some hikers wear a pair of thin liner socks made of polyester and nylon to soak up moisture.

Outdoor Protection

Insects are common in hiking areas. Hikers should frequently apply insect repellent to their clothing to help prevent bites. Long-sleeved shirts, pants, and a hat also can protect hikers from insect bites. Many hikers tuck their pants into their socks.

Hikers often are exposed to a great deal of sunlight. They should apply sunscreen to their skin to prevent sunburn. Hikers often wear sunglasses to protect their eyes. Many hikers wear a hat to shade their face.

Dogs

Some people hike with their dogs. They may attach small packs filled with hiking equipment to their dogs.

Hikers should properly care for their dogs. They should keep their dogs leashed and make sure dogs are allowed in the area. Unleashed dogs can become injured. They also may bother or harm other hikers. Hikers should bring extra water and food for their dogs.

Equipment

- Day pack
- Compass
- Map
- Food
- Water
- First aid kit
- Pocketknife
- Waterproof matches or firestarter
- Insect repellent
- Sunscreen
- Watch
- Whistle
- Flashlight
- Rain gear or extra clothing

CHAPTER 3

Skills and Techniques

Experienced hikers carefully plan their hikes. They look at a map to learn about the area's terrain. They find out about the area's weather and know the forecast. Hikers also decide what type of trails to hike on. Some trails are loop trails. These trails begin and end at the same place. Other trails are linear trails. These trails begin and end at different places.

Hiking Time

Hikers should plan the length of their hike. They should return before dark. Hikers usually allow about 30 minutes for each mile (1.6 kilometers) that they hike. They allow 30 additional minutes for every 1,000 feet (305 meters) of elevation. It

Hikers should know how to read a map before they begin their trip.

is often more difficult to walk up hills than it is to walk on flat land. Hikers adjust these times according to their skill level.

Most hikers allow extra time for the return trip. Hikers may walk slower during the return walk because they are tired.

Stretching

Many hikers stretch before they hike. This activity helps hikers warm up their muscles to prevent injuries. Some hikers also stretch during and after hikes. This stretching can help prevent hikers' bodies from becoming sore. Hikers stretch far enough to feel a gentle pull. They should hold a stretch for about 30 to 60 seconds.

Hikers stretch various body parts. They stretch their legs and lower back. They also stretch their shoulders, neck, arms, and chest.

Terrain

Hikers choose terrain based on their skill and fitness level. Beginning hikers should choose

Steep, rocky areas may be a challenge for hikers.

flat terrain or low hills. This type of terrain usually is easy for hikers to walk on.

Steep hills and mountainsides can be a challenge for hikers. Hikers' feet and knees can quickly become tired. Hikers on hills and mountainsides sometimes walk on switchback trails. These trails follow a zigzag pattern to make it easier for hikers to grip surfaces. On steep slopes, hikers should take small steps.

Reading Topographical Maps

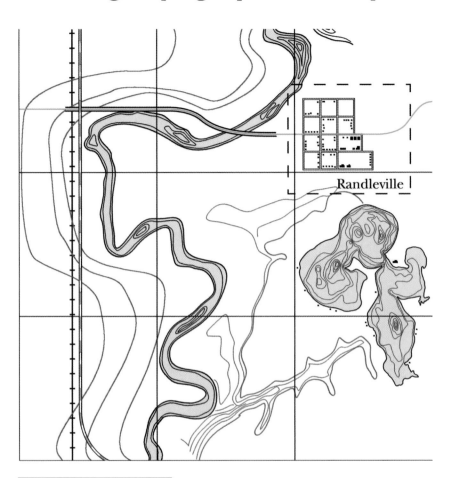

Randleville

Legend	
Contour Line	
Primary Highway	
Secondary Highway	
Railroad	
Bridge	
Water	
House	

Like other maps, topographical maps show features such as rivers, roads, and buildings. But they also use contour lines to show the land's elevation. Widely spaced lines or areas of no lines show level ground. Closely spaced lines show steep slopes.

They should keep their knees relaxed and bent while they hike down steep slopes. These practices help relieve pressure on hikers' legs.

Scree can cause hikers to slip. Hikers on this terrain should move slowly and watch where they step. Hikers may use the edges of their feet to help them grip the terrain.

River gorges can pose dangers to hikers. These deep valleys are located at the sides of rivers. Gorges often have steep, rocky sides and loose gravel. Hikers should not hike in a river gorge during heavy rainfall. The river can rise quickly during these times.

Hikers sometimes need to cross streams. They should only cross streams that are moving slowly. They should look for a wide spot in the stream and cross at an angle moving upstream. These practices help hikers keep their balance.

Hikers should not cross rivers. Rivers often are deep and may have strong currents.

CHAPTER 4

Responsible Hiking

Hikers can cause problems in some hiking areas. Overused trails often erode. The soil on these trails wears away. Hikers sometimes trample plants and harm them. Some hiking areas are becoming polluted. But responsible hikers know how to take care of the environment. They prevent and correct problems that their activity can cause.

Trails

Responsible hikers stay on the trail as much as possible. They walk single file to keep the trail at its original width. They do not wander off either side to avoid mud or rocks on the path. Hikers who leave the trail can destroy plants growing near the trail. They also can make the trail wider or create another trail next to the original one.

Responsible hikers pick up trash that they find along trails.

More people may begin to use the new trail and damage more land.

Hikers may need to step off the trail in certain situations. For example, they may need to allow people on horseback to pass.

Hikers take breaks a distance from the trail. Other hikers then can continue to use the trail. For breaks, hikers should choose areas where they will cause the least amount of damage. They may choose rocky areas or places without plants for breaks.

Hikers often meet other hikers on the trail. Responsible hikers move off to one side of the trail when this happens. They stop walking to let others pass.

Respecting the Environment

Hikers should care for the environment. They should take any trash they create with them. They can dispose of the trash after their hike. Hikers should use resealable packages for food. They should carry water and other beverages in plastic bottles. These bottles often can be sealed and reused.

Hikers can take breaks on large rocks near the trail to prevent damage to plants.

Responsible hikers care for the environment in other ways. They pick up and carry out trash they see along trails. They avoid picking flowers and taking other items found in nature home with them. Members of hiking organizations may add soil to eroded trails to maintain them.

Respecting Wildlife

Animals live in many hiking areas. They usually live away from busy trails. But hikers may see some wildlife on their hikes. Hikers should respect animals' need for food, water, and shelter. Responsible hikers observe animals from behind cover and at a distance. They do not approach animals. This behavior may threaten the animals or scare them away.

Many animals have young during spring. Hikers should be especially respectful during this season. Animals may be more aggressive in spring to protect their young.

Hikers may use binoculars to watch wildlife from a distance.

Responsible hikers do not scatter food or feed animals. Animals may become used to finding food on trails. These animals may lose their natural fear of people. Some of these animals may become aggressive. For example, bears that people feed may try to force food away from people.

Safety

Responsible hikers prepare for unexpected situations. They tell someone about their hiking plans before they leave. Beginning hikers should walk with at least one other person. The other person can get help if an emergency occurs. Hikers should have basic first aid skills to treat injuries.

Weather Safety

Hikers should pay attention to the weather forecast before they begin their hike. They should not hike if thunderstorms are predicted. Hikers should look for signs of approaching storms. For example, they watch the direction in which clouds are moving. A thunderstorm may be approaching if clouds are moving in different directions. Hikers may notice the

Hikers should know how to use the items in their first aid kits.

Hikers should be prepared for heavy rainfall and thunderstorms.

wind die down or feel a sudden rush of cold air before a thunderstorm begins.

Hikers who are caught outside during storms must follow safety guidelines. They should stay away from water sources, tall trees, cliffs, and ridges. Lightning is more likely to strike in these places. Heavy rain can make many hiking areas slippery. Hikers should be careful when they hike after rainfall.

Winter Hiking

Some people hike in winter or during cold weather. These hikers should make sure to keep themselves warm. They need to wear warm clothing such as hats, mittens, scarves, and heavy coats. They should be careful not to become chilled or soaked with sweat. These conditions can cause hypothermia. This condition occurs when a person's body temperature becomes too low. People with hypothermia can become confused and sleepy. They may even die.

Winter hikers also must prevent frostbite. This condition occurs when cold temperatures cause the skin to freeze. These hikers should wear layers of warm clothing that cover their whole bodies. They may protect their face with a ski mask.

Many winter hikers wear a waterproof outside layer of clothing. It is important that hikers' skin remains dry. Wet skin freezes more quickly than dry skin does.

Winter hikers make sure to drink plenty of water and eat often. Food helps keep their energy

Harmful Plants

Poison ivy, poison oak, and poison sumac are three common harmful plants in North America. These plants release an oil that causes a rash to form on the skin. This rash causes the skin to itch. The skin also may swell or form blisters. Hikers should learn to recognize and avoid these plants.

Poison Ivy

Poison ivy usually grows along a red vine. The vines often grow up tree trunks. But poison ivy may form an upright bush if it has nothing to cling to. Poison ivy leaves grow in clusters of three. The leaves vary in length from .3 to 2 inches (7.6 to 51 millimeters). The middle leaf is larger than the outer two. The leaves are red in the spring and shiny green in late spring and summer. The leaves turn orange or red in the fall. The edges of the leaves can be smooth or jagged. In spring and early summer, small yellow-green flowers grow on the vine near the leaf clusters. In late summer, the flowers form white berries. Poison ivy grows throughout most of the United States and southern Canada.

Poison Oak

Poison oak shares many of poison ivy's features. But poison oak almost always grows as a bush. It usually is about 3 feet (.9 meter) tall. Poison oak leaves range from about .5 to 2 inches (13 to 51 millimeters) long. Poison oak's leaves are lobe-shaped. They have rounded notches on their sides. A hairlike growth often covers the plant's leaves, trunk, and berries. Poison oak grows throughout most of the United States and southern Canada.

Poison Sumac

Poison sumac is a large shrub. It can grow as tall as 12 feet (3.6 meters). The plant is green during spring and summer. It turns yellow or red during fall. Pairs of leaves grow opposite one another along a single stem. These leaves may grow up to about 1 foot (.3 meter) long. The top of the stem has a single leaf. One stem usually has seven to 13 leaves. The stem forms yellow-green flowers in spring. It forms clusters of white or pale yellow berries in late summer and early fall. Poison sumac grows in the northernmost and southernmost regions of the United States. It grows best in wet, swampy areas. Poison sumac is common in and around Michigan in the Great Lakes area. It also is common on the southeastern coast of the United States.

Prevention and Treatment

Many hikers wear long pants and long-sleeved shirts to protect themselves from poison ivy, oak, and sumac. Hikers wash their hands and clothes immediately after their hikes. The oil that irritates the skin spreads easily.

Rashes from poison ivy, oak, and sumac usually begin 48 to 72 hours after contact with the skin. Hikers immediately should wash their skin with cold water if they come into contact with one of the plants. They may use creams to help relieve the symptoms. People may see their doctor for severe symptoms.

level high. Hikers need about 1,000 more calories per day in winter than during other seasons.

Animal Safety

Hikers should know how to stay safe around animals. Hikers may encounter other hikers' dogs on trails. These hikers should give the dogs room to pass. Hikers with dogs should control their dogs. They should not hike with dogs in areas where bears live. Many hikers believe that hiking with dogs can increase their chances of bear attacks. The dogs may threaten bears.

Hikers should learn what types of wild animals live in the area. They need to learn how to stay safe around these animals. For example, hikers should back up slowly and look to the side if they encounter a bear at close range. Hikers in areas where venomous snakes are common should only put their hands and feet where they can see them. Snakes sometimes lie underneath rocks or logs. They may strike if they are startled.

Many hikers warn animals of their presence. They talk to others as they walk. They may hum or call out. Hikers may tie small bells to their

Hikers should pay attention to their surroundings as they hike.

packs. Some hikers occasionally thump the ground with a hiking stick to warn snakes of their presence.

Tick Safety

Hikers should try to prevent tick bites. Ticks are small blood-sucking insects that attach themselves to animals and people. Wood ticks and deer ticks are common in North America.

Hikers who become lost can look for landmarks and review the area's map.

Wood ticks may cause Rocky Mountain spotted fever. This disease can cause headaches, muscle aches, and fever. It also can cause a rash on the palms of the hands and soles of the feet. The rash can spread to other parts of the body. In some serious cases, people can die of this illness.

Deer ticks can cause Lyme disease. This disease causes a target-shaped rash around the tick bite. Symptoms of Lyme disease include fever, headache, and muscle soreness.

Hikers should check themselves often for ticks. They may wear tick repellent. Hikers often wear long-sleeved shirts and pants to prevent ticks from reaching the skin.

Safety When Lost

Hikers should pay attention to the trail as they walk. They should look for landmarks such as large rocks. Hikers should stay calm and look for familiar landmarks if they do become lost. They should stay in one place and blow a whistle to alert others.

Groups of hikers may decide on a whistle code. For example, a group may decide two long whistle blows means that someone is lost.

Traffic Safety

Hikers sometimes must walk on roadways with traffic. These hikers should walk single file facing oncoming traffic.

Some hiking trails cross roads with a great deal of traffic. Hikers on these trails should wear brightly colored clothing to help drivers see them.

Safe hikers prevent accidents and are prepared if an accident does occur. These hikers make their outings more enjoyable for themselves and others.

Words to Know

blister (BLISS-tur)—a sore bubble of skin filled with liquid such as water, pus, or blood; blisters often are caused by something rubbing against the skin.

compass (KUHM-puhss)—an instrument people use to find the direction in which they are traveling; compasses have a needle that points north.

erode (i-RODE)—to wear away; overused or neglected trails often erode.

frostbite (FRAWST-bite)—a condition that occurs when cold temperatures freeze skin

gorge (GORJ)—a deep valley with steep, rocky sides

hypothermia (hye-puh-THUR-mee-uh)—a condition that occurs when a person's body temperature becomes too low

polyester (pol-ee-ESS-tur)—a synthetic substance used to make fabric and plastic products

To Learn More

Coppin, Sara. *Hiking: Have Fun, Be Smart.* Explore the Outdoors. New York: Rosen Publishing Group, 2000.

Hooks, Kristine. *Essential Hiking for Teens.* Outdoor Life. New York: Children's Press, 2000.

Thoennes Keller, Kristin. *Camping.* The Great Outdoors. Mankato, Minn.: Capstone High-Interest Books, 2002.

Useful Addresses

American Hiking Society
1422 Fenwick Lane
Silver Spring, MD 20910

Canadian Parks and Recreation Association
216-1600 James Naismith Drive
Gloucester, ON K1B 5N4
Canada

National Park Service Headquarters
1849 C Street NW
Washington, DC 20240

Parks Canada National Office
25 Eddy Street
Hull, QC K1A 0M5
Canada

Internet Sites

American Hiking Society
http://www.americanhiking.org

Backpacker.com
http://www.backpacker.com

**Great Outdoors Recreation Pages—Hiking
   and Backpacking**
http://www.gorp.com/gorp/activity/hiking.htm

National Park Service
http://www.nps.gov

Parks Canada—National Parks
http://www.parkscanada.pch.gc.ca/np/np_e.htm

Index